PUNCH NEEDLE TUTORIAL

The Ultimate Guide on How to Learn Punch Needling for Beginners Including How to Make Punch Needle Projects and Patterns

Boris Joseph

Copyright@2021

TABLE OF CONTENT

CHAPTER 1 3

   INTRODUCTION...3

CHAPTER 3 35

   STEP BY STEP TO MAKE PUNCH NEEDLE
   PROJECT 35

THE END 61

CHAPTER 1

INTRODUCTION

You will require the following tools:

Punch needle tool with threader is a type of needle tool.

Fabric for the foundation

Frame

Yarn

Planned Parenthood (optional)

Scissors

a piece of tape (optional)

Marker with a permanent ink supply

Glue that dries quickly

Punch Needle Tools required

In this case, the most important distinction to make is the distinction between an embroidered punch needle and a yarn thickness punch needle (see below).

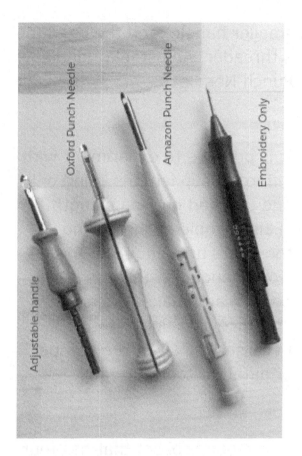

Adjustable handle

Oxford Punch Needle

Amazon Punch Needle

Embroidery Only

Punch Needle with Adjustable
Handle - one tool with six
adjustable loop lengths, a wood
handle, a stainless steel needle,
easy entrance into cloth, a

smaller handle, and the need for a threader. Adjustable Handle Punch Needle

It is possible to experiment with different loop lengths using only one tool and one loop length. It is also simple to thread (no threaders are required), has a wood handle, a stainless steel needle, and makes a smooth entrance into cloth. It is necessary to acquire a number of different tools.

It is a one-tool set that has four adjustable loop lengths and a plastic handle. The needle catches fabric a little (it is still usable but not as enjoyable), the copper needle tarnishes over time, and after some use, the middle portion pops out too easily while working. It is a good tool for beginners because it is inexpensive and simple to use.

Embroidery Punch Needle - This tool is meant for use with small embroidery thread (think cross stitch), since it is too thin to retain yarn. It is intended for use with small embroidery thread (think cross stitch). In addition, it is a wonderful art form, but it should not be utilized while working with yarn.

a Hobby Lobby teal handle Punch Needle (which is not pictured) - one tool with one loop length, plastic handle with a copper needle, needle catches, copper needle tarnishes with time, very simply manufactured.

Fabrics for the foundation

A specific foundation fabric is required for the use of the punch needle. Fabrics purchased from local craft stores or large online fabric retailers (e.g., fabric.com) will not work with the punch needle technique. The needle is too big for most textiles; it will create holes in non-punch needle foundation fabrics and will not keep the yarn in place when used on a normal cloth.

TRADITIONAL LINEN

MONKS CLOTH

RUG WARP

When used as a backdrop, monks cloth is the softest, most malleable material available. It has the smoothest needle entrance, allows fabric strands

9

to flow most freely, and retains yarn the best of any type of fabric (typically project will cover all the fabric)

Because the fabric is attractive, the project does not have to cover the entire space (because the fabric is attractive). Traditional linen (or burlap) is a stiffer material that does not hold yarn as well and allows fabric strands to move more readily.

Rug warp is the same color as Monks cloth, but it is a stiffer fabric that does not retain yarn as well as Monks cloth does.

Frames

1. Wooden embroidery hoops —
a beautiful finished result, but
the fabric is prone to fraying

(this can be fixed by preparing the frame before starting, pulling fabric as tight as possible, trimming fabric and hot gluing to the hoop, if this is done fabric will not slip)

When finished, the work may be transferred to another frame. 2. Plastic no slip embroidery hoops - Holds fabric well, pulls fabric tight, cannot be used to show work after completion (not cost effective and not very attractive), but can be transferred to another frame when completed.

Three. Wooden frames – the
fabric must be stapled or tacked
to the frame; it may be left in
the frame for the duration of the
project; it can also be

transferred to another frame or turned into something else (such as a cushion); the staples or tacks hold the fabric in place securely. In some cases, purchasing an artist painting canvas and removing the canvas material is all that is required to use the wood frame in your project. Hand-assembled stretcher bars are also available, which can be used to support a patient.

4. Carpet tacks are another option. Although not seen in the photo, there are certain frames that employ carpet tack around the borders to hold the fabric in place, but these are often more costly. In the event that you are

up for the challenge, you may create this frame by adding carpet tack to a wooden frame. (For instance, the Oxford Gripper Frame)

Yarn

Is it really necessary to knit with 100 percent wool yarn? No, it is not the case. If you are working on a genuine rug and want to use it as a rug, you should absolutely use 100 percent wool yarn in your project. It is particularly beneficial if you want to make extensive use of your project (i.e. make it into a purse or pillow). For projects other than rugs or purses, you are free to use any yarn you choose! Cotton yarns, acrylic yarns, wool mixes, fancy yarns, and even cut-up pieces of plastic bags and fabric may be used to create a beautiful project.

#5 Bulky

#4 Medium

#6 Super
Bulky

Thickness of the yarn - The thickness of the yarn varies depending on the type of yarn used. Punch needles work best with yarn weights of 4 (medium) or 5 (bulky), according to my experience. I've had varying degrees of success using yarn weight 6. (super bulky). The weights I have are all different. Some of them work OK, some I have to adjust several times while I work (yarn loops are too small and I have to go back), and some won't stay in place at all. For example, I have a gorgeous grey 6 weight yarn that works beautifully and is one of my faves; with that stated, So don't be afraid to try it, but keep in mind that it may not be as simple as you would like it to be. A yarn weight of 7 (jumbo) would be far too heavy and would not work at all in this project. For the opposite end of the spectrum, yarn weights 1(super fine) and 2(fine) will work, but they are extremely thin and take double the amount of punching to fill in the space. My yarn weight is 3 (light), and it works great; but, you must shorten your stitch length (go every 1 or 2 holes in your fabric) in order for the fabric to hold it and for it to fill in properly. Because of this, I prefer to avoid weight 3 whenever possible, although it may work if you find one you enjoy using.

Design

DESIGN OR NO DESIGN?

Is it better to have a design or not? This, I feel, is a matter of personal choice. I didn't want to spend hours trying to find the right pattern for my first item (as I did picking on my yarn colors, lol), so I allowed my heart and intuition guide me through the process, and I absolutely adore the result! I've also had a lot of fun creating pre-made patterns for the kits available in my store. You really can't go wrong either way. Punch needle is a method of creating art with yarn, and I have discovered that yarn is lovely in and of itself on my punch needle adventure. You simply can't go wrong as long as you're working with lovely yarn. Allow your emotions to guide your decision. My one piece of advice is to allow yourself to look ahead just long enough to understand where you want your design to go and to draw a line to guide you. Your foundation fabric includes holes and fabric strands to guide you, but when you pull and tighten the textiles, the lines get distorted and do not always follow a straight line as they should. Drawing your design helps you to follow the pattern you want to achieve rather than depending on the unreliable cloth to lead you through the process of sewing. In my first design, I drew only a few lines and my forms are a little off-kilter.

It's time to throw a punch.

How to Punch Your Way Through Words and Photographs

Following the completion of your design and the preparation of your frame, it's time to begin punching. To begin, thread the punch needle tool with a fine thread.

To thread the needle, thread it using a threading wire. Insert the needle threader into the top of the needle and tighten the threader.

Using the threader, thread the punch needle tool through the top of the tool.

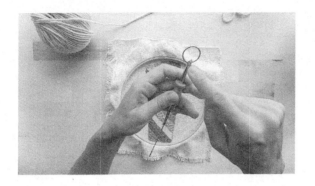

2 inches of yarn should be
threaded through the threader
loop end.

Pull the threader and yarn
through the needle one more
time.

Pulling a loop of yarn through the eye of the punch needle is a simple process. Pull the yarn through the hole.

Make a loop of yarn and feed it through the eye of a punch needle.

Notches may be used to alter the length of the punch needle to accommodate varied loop lengths. Simply twist the needle, pull or push it to the appropriate length, and then spin it to secure it in place with a lock.

When utilizing an Oxford Punch Needle tool, it is important to understand how to thread it. Watch the video below to discover how.

In the case of a design that has little detailed regions (for example, the eyes of an animal), begin with such parts first. If your design is straightforward, with vast spaces to fill (as in my work), you can begin anywhere you choose in the process. I started with the dark copper yarn on the outside edge of the square.

Begin in the centre of your outline and work your way out. The tail end will protrude if you begin near the edge; it will also be more likely to come undone over time.

Begin punching in the centre of your design area and work your way out.

For the first row around the outline, use a small stitch length to ensure that the outline is clearly visible. In your Monks cloth, a short stitch is approximately every 2 holes.

The first row of punch needles is a close stitch every two holes in the cloth on the first row.

Insert the needle until the wooden handle of the needle hits the canvas. Pull the needle out of the hole and move it across two holes. Make certain that the needle's open slot is pointed in the direction in which you are operating. Also, be sure you graze the cloth with the point of your needle.

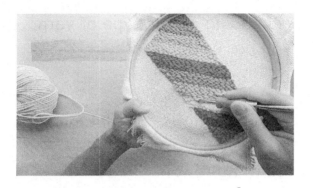

Each time the punch needle handle comes into contact with the cloth

If you elevate the needle point too high, you will get loops on the reverse side of the fabric.

Having completed the first row outline all the way around, you will open up your stitch for the remainder of the row and continue working. A bigger stitch will be every 3-5 holes, depending on the type of yarn you are working with.

The initial punch needle row is offset by one row in the following row.

You'll want to punch in the middle of your mountain peak from the first row for your second row to make it easier to see. Due to the fact that you are opening up your stitch, you will be able to reach every other mountain top.

As you work, double-check your work. If there are any bare

places, move the punches closer to one another.

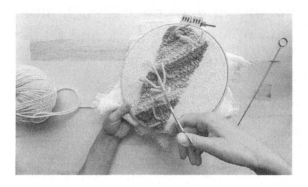

If this is your first time punching, don't be intimidated by all of the technicalities. It is considerably less difficult than it appears. I've learnt to use a close stitch for the outline and bigger stitches for the subsequent rows during the course of my knitting career. It contributes to the overall aesthetic appeal of the design. However, it is not required. I urge that you just get started.

You will succeed if you graze your needle and contact the handle of your needle each time. You may also go back and fill in the blanks afterwards.

In order to turn corners, it is easiest to spin the frame in your hands as you get to a tight curve. While leaving your needle in the fabric, continue punching and rotating the piece while also turning the needle, making sure the open slot of your needle is facing the direction in which you are working, and leaving your needle in the fabric.

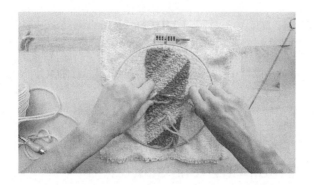

There are no knots required to finish each color! Make a long loop with the needle by punching it to the long loop side. Pull a tiny loop out of the fabric and trim it.

Trim the tail of the punch needle tool once it has been punched to the front side of the cloth.

Remove the Punch Needle tool from the fabric, leaving a short tail on the loop side of the tool.

The end result will be a slew of small tiny tails scattered throughout your design once you have finished all of the colors. Simply cut these tails so that they blend in with the rest of the loops on the hook.

Trim any stray yarn bits that may have gotten away from you as well. The cloth will maintain its shape

CHAPTER 3

STEP BY STEP TO MAKE PUNCH NEEDLE PROJECT

Punch needle is having a comeback in the yarn crafts industry. It is a method that sits midway between needlework and rug-making, with designs spanning from highly abstract to very intricate; utilizing a variety of threads from thick yarn to embroidery floss.

In this lesson, we examine the method of needle punching on a small embroidery hoop and with a fine needle. Although this discipline can expose some difficulties, it is primarily a soothing art, and the few ideas that follow will hopefully leave you hungry for more.

Here you will learn beginning techniques needed to make your own punch needle patterns; you may also opt to follow along and utilize the lovely "Significant Otter" pattern supplied in Step 1.

Supplies

- a 10cm diameter embroidery hoop

- embroidery thread in light
blue, red, black, and 3 tones of
brown (or other colours your
design asks for) (or whichever
colours your design calls for)

- a 1.3mm adjustable punch
needle; the one used here is
from Rico

- scrap cloth, thick enough to
grab the thread (denim is used
in this example) (denim is used
in this example)

- fray stop

- scissors, pen or fabric marker, paper, tracing paper

Step 1: Create Your Design

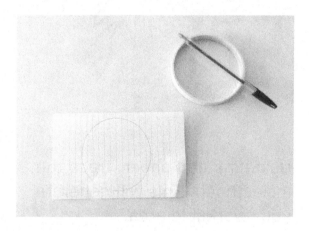

Design: Lily_2point0

Using ink and paper, trace the inside hoop. This will generate your workable area.

It is worth noting, with punch needle designs, that you will prefer geometric forms, or solid colour sections, as extremely minute details might be lost amid the loops.

One you're done, go to the next stage.

Alternatively, download and print the Significant Otter design file supplied below.

Step 2: Prepare Your Hoop

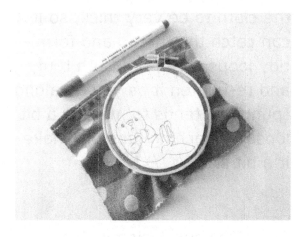

Add the scrap fabric to the
embroidery hoop; you will want
the cloth to be very thick, so it
can catch the thread and form
tidy loops. Keep the cloth taut,
and re-tighten it as you go along
(punching tends to make it a bit
loose) (punching tends to make
it a bit slack.)

Transfer your design with a
fabric marker, either by cutting
it out, using tracing paper, or -

if you have a projector - projecting it onto the fabric.

Once you have two strands of black embroidery floss threaded through the punch needle tool, you may proceed to reading the punch needle suggestions that are provided below.

Note: if excessively thick, there is a risk that the thread may get stuck in the needle and will halt the loops forming, delaying any progress. Always test the thickness of thread for your size needle in a tiny section of the hoop. This may be unravelled before commencing the real design.

Step 3: Punch Needle Tips

There are 2 approaches, and 2 results you can achieve using punch needles.

A typical one is to work on the wrong side of the cloth to generate a dense loop effect on the right side. The impact can also change depending on the length of the loop. The alternative, is to work in continuous stitches, that will seem similar to embroidered back-stitches. In such instance, start by sketching the form you intend to fill in and move around toward the centre.

How to work

To start punching, thread the tool with a needle threader: first through the pen, then through the eye of the needle. Then, puncture the cloth and grab the end of the thread coming from the eye of the needle. You may modify the quantity by tugging the other end of the thread, coming out of the top of the punch needle (care out, you don't want to pull too much and unthread it!).

Then, carefully take up the pen, brush the surface of the fabric, and punch again. Repeat the procedure, producing loops on the underside of the cloth. Always work with the large hole

of the needle facing the
direction of progress.

Be careful not to hold the hoop
too near to oneself and get
unintentionally stabbed, these
instruments are sharp!

Tips & fixes

Do not take the needle off the
cloth too much, you could cause
some unravelling. If that's the
case, bring the punch needle
vertically back to the last secure
stitch and carefully draw the
thread coming out of the top
until the needle hits the cloth.
Resume punching from there.

If you have produced holes in the fabric due to unravelling, simply massage the area between your fingers until they disappear. This will make the cloth "catchy" again and prevent stitches from being undone.

Once you've worked a thread, cut the extremities to fit the loop length, particularly if doing loops on the right side.

Step 4: Design Contour

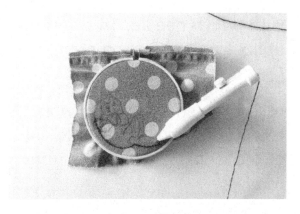

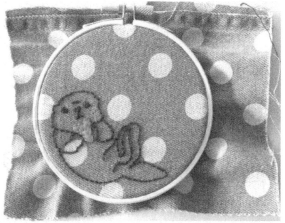

As we've just shown in the tips,
there are 2 approaches, and 2
different effects we can obtain

with punch needle. This design utilizes a combination of both.

The otter contour and heart will utilize the straight stitch while the interior region will take use of the loops to produce a fluffy otter.

Start by evenly contouring in black. Remember to alway have the big hole of the needle pointing in the direction of progress. It might help to flip the whole hoop as you go along and observe your work sideways.

Once the otter is done, thread 2 strands of crimson and fill the heart. Start by tracing its shape, and fill it in by walking around the inside until you reach the centre.

Step 5: Filling In

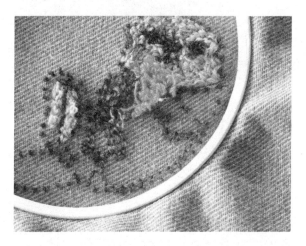

To fill the colours in, we'll punch on the wrong side of the cloth, making loops on the right side. If you have an adjustable punch needle, you may alter the loop length for each colour. For the otter, we'll divide them down as follows:

- head and beneath feet: light brown/beige

- body: brown

- tail: dark brown

Because we're using such thin thread, it is possible that we'll have to go over stitches several times on the wrong side, to produce additional loops on the front. If you desire to keep your fabric from showing through the gaps, we'd recommend painting the spots with brown fabric paint beforehand.

To fill the colour in, start by contouring the area you wish to fill on the incorrect side, verifying that you're not crossing the black outlines on the front. Then, work around the inside of the area towards the middle. Check the quantity of loops on the right side and repeat as required, beginning from the outline.

When your otter is filled in, check the right side to verify if the black outlines are still visible. If need be, go over them again with a longer stitch setting (especially for face, arms, and legs details) (particularly for face, arms, and legs details).

Step 6: Writing

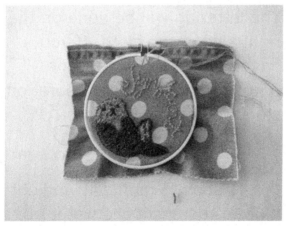

The lettering will be done on the right side of the cloth. If you haven't transferred the word onto the hoop in the preparation stage, do it now.

We'll punch "Significant" in light blue to represent the water our otter may be drifting in. If you're following your own design and desire to add writing, make sure you choose a typeface where letters are linked, to make it easier to punch in one go.

Before you start, think out which is the best path to take to prevent cutting thread between letters; that might mean beginning at the end. In this example, we start at the top of the "S", all the way up to the tail, then double-up the thread until the center, where the leg of the I starts, and follow along to the end of the "t", omitting the dots on the "i"s.

If you want, this stage can also be embroidered using a back-stitch.

Dot the eyes with French knots (three loops around the needle should make them thick enough) (three wraps around the needle should make them thick enough).

Step 7: Finishing Off

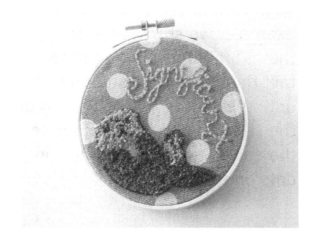

To secure your stitches, apply
some fray stop to the back of
the hoop, particularly where

threads end and start. Try to additionally block certain loops from the contour and and writing. Let it dry.

Finish the hoop as you would other embroidery projects: you could choose to sew the extra fabric and add a backing, or trim the borders and fold the fabric on the inside of the hoop, fixing it with a hot glue gun. The finishing process is completely up to you.

Add a thread or ribbon at the top, and your first punch needle creation is ready to hang proudly on your wall!

THE END

Made in the USA
Coppell, TX
07 January 2025

44097386R00036